TALKING ABOUT
Bullying

Bruce Sanders

Franklin Watts
London • Sydney

© Aladdin Books Ltd 2003

Designed and produced by
Aladdin Books Ltd
28 Percy Street
London W1T 2BZ

First published in Great Britain
in 2003 by
Franklin Watts
96 Leonard Street
London EC2A 4XD

ISBN: 0 7496 5392 2

Design: Flick, Book Design and Graphics

Picture research: Brian Hunter Smart

The consultant, Michele Elliott, is director
of Kidscape, a children's charity helping
the parents of bullied or bullying children.

The publishers would like to
acknowledge that the photographs
reproduced in this book have been
posed by models or have been obtained
from photographic agencies.

A CIP record for this book is available
from the British Library.

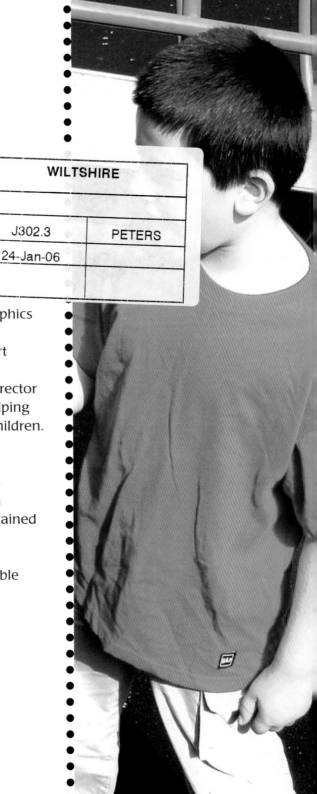

Contents

"Why should we talk about bullying?"

Bullying is a problem that affects many children. When a bully says, "I'm going to get you after school", it can make the person they are picking on worried or scared.

Because of bullies, some children feel afraid to go into the playground, the lunchroom or the toilets. Some are so terrified they even skip school to avoid the bullies.

This book talks about what bullying is, who does it and why it happens.

If you are being bullied, it may help you to think about ways of protecting yourself.

If you are bullying someone, this book may help you to realise what you are doing.

Bullying should *never* be ignored. If someone you know is being bullied, tell an adult.

Did you know...

Having bullies around takes the fun out of school. Bullying bothers everyone, not just the children who are getting picked on.

"What is bullying?"

When they hear the word "bully", many people think of someone who hits others or pushes them around. But a bully can hurt other people in lots of ways.

Bullying can be shouting at people, calling them names, damaging their things, saying nasty things behind their back, or making them feel left out.

Bullying is *always* the bullies' fault, not the person they are picking on.

Sadly, bullying doesn't only happen in the playground at school: it happens in families, at clubs and at work.

If you are being bullied, you can do something about it.

Talk to an adult you trust. Explain what is going on, and talk to them about what you would like to be done.

Did you know...

Here are some ways that bullies pick on other people:

- Hitting or pushing them
- Picking on them because of their colour or religion
- Calling them names
- Spreading nasty rumours about them
- Making them feel left out
- Forcing them to hand over money or possessions

"Who is a bully?"

Anyone can be a bully if they try to hurt or upset others, or deliberately make other people look foolish or stupid.

Girls and boys, and even adults, can be bullies. Some bullies have had bad things happen to them at home. They are cruel to others because they are unhappy.

Some bullies have
been bullied themselves, but
that is no excuse to hurt others.

Not all bullies are bigger and stronger than the people they bully, but they use threats to scare people. Other bullies get together in a gang to pick on others.

Some people are good at making clever remarks and can be very hurtful just by the things they say.

Think about it

We can all be a bit of a bully at times. Have you snatched a toy from a younger brother, or said something mean to a shy classmate?

This is different to people who are bullies most of the time: people who are always making life miserable for others. Is there anyone you are always mean to?

"Where does bullying happen?"

People get bullied in lots of different places, but most bullying takes place in and around school: in the playground, in the toilets, or on the school bus.

Bullies usually pick places and occasions where there are no adults around, so they won't get caught. They hope that other children are too afraid to say anything.

Some bullies act like angels in front of the teacher, but as soon as the teacher has left the room, they start picking on someone in the class.

My story

"My Dad said, 'Why don't you just fight back'. But it's not that simple. This guy in my class is really sneaky. He says things quietly so the teacher can't hear. When I react, I'm the one who gets caught. Now the teacher thinks I'm the troublemaker."
Paul

Bullies wait until there are no adults around. They rely on the fact that other children won't report them.

"Why pick on me?"

When someone starts to bully you, you may wonder what you have done. You may feel upset or wonder if there is something wrong with you. But it isn't you. It's the bully that is wrong.

Bullies have a problem. They will always find a reason to pick on someone else.

Don't believe anything a bully says. It is the bully who has the problem.

Bullies may say mean things about how someone looks, about their intelligence or the colour of their skin.

Bullies also make up things to pick on people. They do not care if what they say is true or not. They just want to make other people miserable.

Did you know...

Racist bullying and name calling happen to many children in schools. Bullies have learned this hurtful behaviour from others. They want to make out they are better by putting others down.

If anyone is behaving like this, it is really important to let your parents and your teacher know.

"What does it feel like to be bullied?"

Bullying may make you feel scared and upset. It may also make you feel lonely and unpopular, or that you're no good.

Bullies can make you so worried that you can't think about anything else. Being bullied also gives some children very bad nightmares.

If you are being bullied, don't blame yourself — ever!

Being bullied can also make you angry and frustrated. You know it isn't fair but you're not sure what to do about the bullying or who to tell.

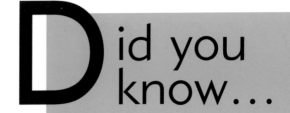

Did you know...

Adults can and do bully children. They may do it by making them feel bad in front of other people or by teasing or making fun of them.

It can be hard to know what to do if an adult in your family or in school bullies you.

Adults should never bully kids, so find someone to tell if this is happening to you. Try talking to another adult, a family friend or a teacher you trust.

"What is wrong with gangs?"

It can be exciting to be in a gang, playing or hanging out in a group and sharing secrets. However, bullying often takes place when people get into groups. Some groups torment other people for no good reason, to make themselves feel better or stronger.

Children may go along with the bully in a gang to avoid being picked on.

Sometimes you get on fine with someone when you're on your own with them. But when they are with a particular group of children, they turn nasty and spiteful.

That's the problem with gangs – people may go along with the bully in the gang to avoid being picked on themselves.

Think about it

If you are in a gang, think about what it gets up to:

• Does your gang pick on people?
• If so, why do you enjoy being in the gang?
• Are you ever afraid of being picked on yourself?
• Who could you talk to about things you don't like in the gang?
• How can you get out of the gang?

"Why do bullies do it?"

Bullies usually want other people to notice them. They want to show off and to feel bigger and better than other people.

They think the best way to do this is to hurt others or make them feel small.

Bullies frighten people into being nice to them. But nobody really likes a bully.

They may not show it, but many bullies are actually unhappy inside.

Sometimes they are just jealous of other people, so they try to upset them or spoil their fun.

My Story

"When I got home my big brother always picked on me. I hated it. At school the next day, I'd pick on someone else smaller than me. It made me feel better at the time, but I guess I was a bully too, just like my brother."
Amy

"Who can help?"

Though you can stop bullies by yourself or with your friends' help, the best way to stop bullying is to tell an adult. Don't be afraid to ask. Everyone needs help at times.

Tell an adult that you trust. It could be your Mum or Dad, or anyone you know who cares about you. Most parents will do whatever they can to help you.

Don't be afraid to ask for help. Talk to an adult you trust.

But what if the person you tell doesn't help? Or what if your parents don't do anything to help after you've told them?

Don't give up. Tell another adult you trust, like a friend's parent you know well or your class teacher.

 **My Story**

"My big sister was always saying I was fat and ugly. When I complained to Mum, she said, 'Ignore her, she's just teasing.'

Things got worse and worse. In the end, I spoke to my teacher. She had a word with my Mum, who was shocked. She hadn't realised how upset I'd been. She had a chat with my sister and things are much better now."

Danielle

"Should I tell on bullies?"

Telling an adult about bullies or bullying isn't "telling tales". No one should be bullied or made to suffer in silence. Are you afraid to tell on a bully? Perhaps you are scared that the bullying will get worse or that the bully will pick on you instead. Did you know that many schools stop the bullying without the bully ever knowing who told them about the problem?

Even if the bully finds out, it is best to get things out in the open. If you keep quiet, the bullying can go on for years.

Other children often have good ideas about how to stop bullying.

Think about it

Class discussions can help to bring things into the open. If teachers know that lots of children are feeling unhappy, they can work with you to have a school policy on bullying.

When everyone begins to express and share their feelings about life at school, it gets easier to talk if someone is making you unhappy.

"What about bullying at our school?"

You may be worried about what will happen if you tell your teachers, even if it is someone else who is being bullied. However, if you do tell, you are helping to stop the bully from getting away with it and teachers are usually glad to be told. If you have any friends who have seen what is going on, ask if they will support you.

Most adults, including parents and teachers, will listen and try to help.

Many schools have already thought about how to deal with bullies.

Some teachers in your school may already be trained to talk to bullies and their families.

Talk about it

Do you know someone who is being bullied? Don't ignore bullying. There are simple ways you can help:

• Don't try to take the bully on.

• Refuse to join in, and try to be a friend to the person being bullied.

• Tell an adult what is going on.

• Sometimes bullying happens outside school. Do the teachers in your school know this?

"What else can I do?"

Your school may ignore bullying, or perhaps you're being bullied outside school.

Here are five things that Kidscape recommends if you are being bullied:

① Try to ignore the bully – say "No" angrily, then turn and walk away.

② Try not to show that you are upset – bullies want to see you cry or look afraid.

Try telling the bully to stop. Just put up your hand and say "no" angrily.

③ Don't fight back if you can help it. You could make things worse, or get blamed for starting the trouble.

④ Stick with friends. Bullies tend to pick on people who are on their own.

⑤ Think up clever replies. To give yourself confidence, you could practise them in front of the mirror at home.

Remember, it's always best to tell an adult what is going on – you need their help.

Did you know...

The best way to stop a gang bullying you is to tell someone about it. You could also try talking to members of the gang on their own. Ask them why they are ganging up on you.

Some bullies are only brave in front of their friends. Talk to the bully in the gang on their own and ask them to stop picking on you.

"What if I'm a bully?"

Being a bully makes some people feel big and strong, or "cool" in front of the gang.

But many bullies do not realise how much they hurt other people when they pick on them.

Others may also be worried that if they don't join in, they might be bullied too.

If you are always picking on other people, then you have a problem. But you can change.

Think about why you bully others. Do you really mean to hurt them? Or is something else making you miserable?

Are you being bullied yourself? If so, it's very important that you tell someone you trust.

Try to say sorry. It's not easy, but it is an important thing to do.

You decide

You can try some of these things if you want to stop bullying. If you don't get rid of the bullying habit, you could have problems when you are older.

• When you feel angry, try not to take it out on others. Go for a walk or hit a pillow if you feel really mad.

• Try to say sorry to people you have bullied. They may not believe you at first, but keep on trying.

• If you find it hard to sit still at school all day, take up a new hobby. It is also a great way to make new friends.

Why bullying matters

• Bullying is always mean, whether it is pushing someone around, calling them names or making them feel left out.

• Some people think that bullying is just part of life. It isn't. No one deserves to be bullied, and bullying should never be ignored.

• Bullies who get away with it grow up thinking that being mean to others is a good way to behave. They just turn into big bullies.

• Bullying should always be stopped. The best way to deal with bullies at school or at home is to tell an adult.

Life without bullies is a lot more fun for everyone.

Books about Bullying

If you want to read more about bullying, try:

All About Bullying by Leslie Ely (Hodder)
How Do I Feel About Bullies and Gangs
by Julie Johnson (Franklin Watts)
I Feel Bullied by Jen Green (Hodder Wayland)
The Bullybusters Joke Book by John Byrne
(Red Fox)
Picking on Percy by Cathy MacPhail
(Barrington Stoke)

Useful addresses and phone numbers

If you can't talk to someone close to you, then
try ringing one of these organisations. They
have been set up to help you:

Childline
Tel: 0800 1111
A 24-hour free helpline for children. This
number won't show up on a phone bill.

Kidscape
2 Grosvenor Gardens
London SW1W 0DP
Tel: 020 7730 3300 (Mon–Fri 10 am–4 pm)
A helpline for parents of bullied or bullying
children. Send a large SAE for copies of booklets.

On the Web

These websites are also helpful. You can get in
touch with some of them using email:

www.childline.org.uk
www.kidscape.org.uk
www.kidshealth.org
www.bullying.org
www.kidshelp.com.au

NSPCC (National
Society for Prevention
of Cruelty to Children)
Tel: 0800 800 500
A 24-hour free helpline for
anyone worried about bullying.

Kids Helpline, Australia
Tel: 1800 55 1800
A 24-hour free helpline for children.

ParentLink, Australia
Tel: 02 6205 8800
A confidential helpline offering advice for
parents of bullied or bullying children.

You can also find out about how to stop bullies on the internet.

Index

Photocredits
Abbreviations: l-left, r-right, b-bottom, t-top, c-centre, m-middle
All photos supplied by PBD except for:
Front cover, 8, 9, 12, — Digital Vision. 6, 20, 21 — Corbis. 10, 11, 25, 30 — Brand X Pictures. 13, 14 — Select Pictures. 24 — Roger Vlitos.